# The Octopus
# *and*
# Other Cephalopods

*by Gladys Conklin*

HOLIDAY HOUSE · NEW YORK

*For Polly Fry and her family*

Copyright © 1977 by Gladys Conklin
All rights reserved
Printed in the United States of America

*Library of Congress Cataloging in Publication Data*

Conklin, Gladys Plemon.
 The octopus and other cephalopods.

 Bibliography: p. 59
 Includes index.
 SUMMARY: Describes the characteristics and
habits of the octopus, squid, argonaut, and other
cephalopods, that class of mollusks having a mantle,
tentacles, and the ability to change color.
 1. Cephalopoda—Juvenile literature.
[1. Cephalopods.  2. Octopus.  3. Squid]
I. Title.
QL430.2.C59      594       77-3818
ISBN 0-8234-0306-8

# Contents

CO. SCHOOLS
C860355

*Acknowledgment*

Many books were read to acquire a feeling of knowing the fascinating cephalopods. I am especially grateful to Jacques Cousteau and Philippe Diolé, not only for the wealth of information in their book *Octopus and Squid: The Soft Intelligence*, but also because Cousteau and his men demonstrate the friendliness, the grace, and the beauty of these colorful creatures.

G.C.

# One

# What Are Cephalopods?

Mollusks are animals with shells but without backbones. They are part of the great group of backboneless animals, the invertebrates, that include insects, spiders, worms, crabs, and many others. Mollusks themselves are an enormous group—there are more than 100,000 kinds of them.

Cephalopods are a class of mollusks that contains the largest, fastest, and perhaps the most mysterious of all the invertebrates; among the invertebrates, they are the most complicated in structure and behavior. They include the octopus, the squid, the cuttlefish, the pearly nautilus, the argonaut, the spirula, and the extinct ammonoids. Many ages ago they filled the seas. In comparison, today there are only a few remaining species. They are marine animals, and the fossil records seem to show that they have always been so.

The cephalopods are the most highly developed and some are the most intelligent of all invertebrate animals. They have unusually large brains in proportion to the size of their bodies. Their sense organs are well developed, and large eyes are usual. Their mouths have black, horny beaks shaped a little like a parrot's beak. This rips food into small pieces and is also used to break open shells of other mollusks.

All cephalopods have a mantle—a sort of loose cape —that covers the body. It is generally unattached near the head, but in the octopus it grows closely into the head on three sides. A short tube called a funnel sticks out under the head. By closing its mantle, the animal can squirt the gathered water out of the funnel. This moves the cephalopod rapidly, by a form of jet propulsion. By changing the direction of the funnel, it can go backward, forward, or in any other direction. It can get around more quickly and efficiently than any other kind of mollusk— dramatically different from such relatives as the ponderously moving clam.

The "foot" of other mollusks is usually a broad, muscular pad such as that on which a snail moves. In the cephalopods it has changed through evolution to form the tentacles and the funnel.

Every cephalopod has tentacles, which are long and very flexible organs that grow out next to its head. There may be dozens of tentacles on a pearly nautilus and just eight (usually called arms in this case) on an octopus. They catch food and are in some cases used for walking about on rocks.

## Color Changers

One of the most remarkable things about cephalopods is that they can change their color instantly. Many of the

All mollusks have a "foot"; in the cephalopods it evolved into tentacles. These two pictures of the Atlantic oval squid show them closed, above, and separated as the squid reacts to the diver's hand at left in what is thought to be a threat posture of the cephalopod. ABOVE, WOMETCO MIAMI SEAQUARIUM; BELOW, JOHN LIDINGTON

color changes help them to disappear into their background by camouflage. There are very small spots of pigment throughout the entire surface of the cephalopod, each in a small sac that is transparent. Minute strands of muscle are attached to each sac. By stretching these little muscles the animal widens the sacs and the color is seen; when it relaxes the muscles, the sacs close and the color all but disappears. Each sac is controlled by its own nerve, and a great variety of patterns can appear on the skin.

Cephalopods of today no longer have external shells, except for the pearly nautilus and the argonaut. Instead there is a small shell inside the body. The lack of protection by a shell has forced them to be quick and alert, and they have thus developed into the fastest and most intelligent of the invertebrates.

The name of their class is Cephalopoda. This is from the Greek *kephale*, "head," and *pod*, meaning "foot"—the animals that have their heads united with their "feet," or tentacles.

# Two

# The Strange and Wonderful Octopus

The octopus is a clever animal, and a graceful one. From years of a bad reputation in books and stories that pictured it as a horrible and dangerous monster, many people think of it with a shudder. But if they knew it as it really is in the sea, their feelings would turn to admiration.

This animal is the most widely known of the cephalopods. It is found in all the oceans from tropical waters to the frigid arctic seas. Some octopuses are only two inches across when they are fully grown. The common species, *Octopus vulgaris*, is the one most generally known. It may reach about three meters (about 10 feet) in its span (the body with arms stretched out on both sides) when it is fully grown, and weigh about 25 kilograms, or about 55 pounds. Usually, however, it is somewhat smaller.

Most octopuses are very timid. Their attacks are aimed mainly at the crabs and other crustaceans that, along with shellfish, are their food. They will usually avoid human divers if they can; if an octopus touches one, the diver has only to remain still and the animal will usually

9

*A giant octopus of the Pacific Ocean. Its arms are spread as it climbs a rocky wall, showing the webbing between them. The left eye is seen, almost closed. Octopuses are a little confusing to look at, not only because of the eight arms but also because the body itself suggests a large snout. This octopus is facing left; the arms extend from the head area, which accounts for the word "cephalopod."*

lose interest. If the diver fights, the octopus will hold on as a matter of self-defense.

There are giant octopuses in the Pacific Ocean. One of these giants can weigh over 50 kilograms (over a hundred pounds) and measure nine meters (about 30 feet) in length. Formerly octopuses were thought to be the largest cephalopods, but the still bigger giant squid now has that honor.

Ages ago the octopus had a protective shell and gradually lost it in the course of evolution. But it is clever at escaping the dangers of the sea as well as those from human beings. It has excellent eyesight, with two large, dark eyes. When it is in danger, it can change not only its color but also its shape. The change of shape helps disguise it and allows it to slip into a narrow hole in the rocks. It can also let out a jet of black "ink" and disappear behind the cloud this creates in the water. The octopus has a highly developed sense of touch, in some ways more delicate than that of humans, and this enables it to handle objects in building a home.

An octopus has eight arms, and on the common species the underside of each arm is covered with two rows of suckers. These suckers help the animal to catch and hold food, and are used also to attach itself to a secure base, such as a rock or the sides of the hole it arranges for itself in a pile of rocks.

A web stretches from one arm to another near the head. This web waves back and forth when the octopus is moving slowly over the bottom of the sea. As the tip of each arm touches the bottom, the effect suggests an underwater ballet dancer. While swimming freely in the sea, the octopus is equally beautiful in movement.

## Building a Home

For a large adult, the favorite habitat is under a pile of big, flat rocks in water some 9 meters (about 30 feet) deep. If rocks are not available, the octopus can build its own home. It can pick up bottles, bits of metal, even old tires, and heap them into a pile. It may even dig a hole under the pile to make itself a fully suitable home.

Though it has adopted a life of crawling around on the bottom of the sea—where it pulls itself along from seaweed to rocks by using its suckers—it needs this "house" for defense against its particular enemies, moray and conger eels and large fish called groupers. However, it doesn't remain in one house very long. In a day or two it may go out looking for food and never return. A new home can be found almost any place.

## All Kinds of Colors

Many sea creatures can change their color. The octopus is a master at being able to change its appearance and do it quickly. When at peace with its surroundings, it is some shade of brown to match the sand or rocks beneath it, or of green to match the seaweed where it is hiding. When the creature is excited or disturbed, the color will change quickly, almost in a flash. It turns white when it is frightened and bright red when angry. There

*This dwarf octopus is investigating a broken sea-snail shell; being very flexible, octopuses can slide easily into small holes. Note the funnel, or siphon, below its eye. Cephalopods have eyes with adjustable pupils, as we do, but in many species the pupil assumes an uneven shape when it becomes smaller.*

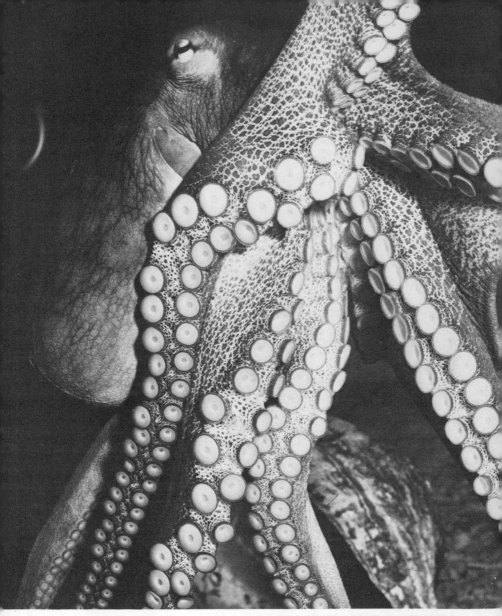

*Suction cups, or suckers, on the arms give an octopus great skill in climbing over rocks and catching prey.*

may be a display of swiftly changing colors from dull red to shades of blue.

Frequently an octopus will settle on the bottom where the sand is light brown, plants a deep green, and coral is red. It will instantly take on a varied color pattern and seem to disappear.

The octopus is a shy animal and leads a solitary life. When it is disturbed, it quickly disappears into the first available hole or crevice. It can flow into a crack in the rocks so small that it is hardly visible. It is able to stretch itself thin, like rubber, and pass through an opening that seems impassable. It can do this because it has no skeleton.

Some octopuses have the ability to cast off an arm when they are caught. The arm breaks off automatically, as the tails of some lizards do when they are captured. The lizard regrows its tail, and the octopus produces another arm.

An octopus likes shallow water, as little as a meter or so (three or four feet) deep. It also likes calm water, and at the approach of a storm will go down as deep as 24 or 30 meters (about 80 or 100 feet).

### Food and Venom

There is plenty of food available. Crabs are the most popular item in the octopus diet; also lobsters and shrimps, clams, oysters, and many kinds of fish. One might think that a live oyster or clam would be too difficult to open. But that's one way an octopus uses the suckers on its arms. It fastens a number of suckers on both sides of the shellfish and pulls steadily in opposite directions. The shell slowly opens and the octopus has a feast.

Because it is so available, crabmeat makes up most of the diet. The powerful beak of an octopus can easily crush a crab's shell. Sometimes it injects venom into the crab and quickly makes it helpless. Every bit of the crab's flesh is eaten, even the meat inside the jointed legs.

The venom of an octopus is produced by two glands not far from its beak. The poison kills a crab or other crustacean almost immediately. In the case of smaller octopuses it does a human being little damage, causing only some reddening and swelling of the skin around the bite. Large octopuses, however, have large, strong beaks and inject more venom. And there is one species in the waters of Australia, called the blue-ringed octopus, whose venom is very powerful and causes human death.

The octopus has many enemies besides groupers and eels. They include sharks, whales, seals, and various large fish. It is easy for the thin and slippery eels to invade the tunnels, rock piles, and caves that octopuses hide in. The moray eel is a strong, quick animal with sharp teeth. Though it has poor eyesight, its sense of smell is highly developed.

If a moray and an octopus meet out in open water, the octopus will immediately shoot off by jet propulsion. Probably it also will add a squirt of ink. The moray can still follow the octopus by odor and soon catches up. A fierce battle results.

The moray grasps one of the arms of the octopus in its powerful jaws while the octopus covers the moray with its numerous suckers. The moray bites and twists and sweeps the grasping arms from its body time after time. The moray can do this because its body is covered with a thick coating of slime. It is likely to tie itself literally into a knot and then pull its head back through the loop; this often results in dislodging one or two of the cephalopod's arms.

Or sometimes the octopus will break away, leaving most of one arm in the moray's mouth. This doesn't cripple the octopus, for it can grow itself a new arm. More often one of the fighters will die; probably it will be the octopus. A swift eel bite on top of the head will do it.

## Mating

An octopus lives half of its rather short life before it starts hunting for a mate. The ocean offers a vast area in which to hide and the male often has a long search before he finds a female. When the hunt is over and the female shows she is willing, the two of them spend some time caressing each other with their arms. The male may change color from a reddish brown to a light blue when the female has indicated her readiness to mate.

A male carries sperms to the female's eggs in one of his arms. It is the third one on his right. One suction disk is about twice as large as any of the other disks; this identifies the octopus as a male. After caressing the female's body, the male stretches out his sex arm and reaches inside her mantle cavity. He places packets of sperms near the egg tube.

The mating usually lasts about one hour but can extend to several hours. Both animals seem completely absorbed in one another. When the mating is completed, the female pushes the male away. Her whole interest now is the care of her eggs. The female will mate only once in her lifetime. The male may mate with other females during the mating season, however.

## Clusters of Eggs

It may be three weeks or as long as two months before the female lays her eggs. She chooses a dark cave in the rocks. As the eggs come from the egg tube, they are fertilized by the sperms placed there by the male. The eggs are very small, about three millimeters, or an eighth of an inch, long, and the female fastens them in clusters on the rocks.

She broods her eggs with great care. She keeps them covered with her body and squirts water over them with her funnel. This gives them additional oxygen and helps keep them clean. She also uses her suckers for cleaning sand, dirt, and parasites from the eggs.

The females are usually on guard for 24 hours a day and don't eat while they are caring for their eggs. Many

*A cluster of eggs from a giant Pacific octopus. The infant cephalopods are nearly ready to hatch. In the indented part of the cluster at top left, one in particular shows rather clearly; the two eyes near its front and the pigment spots can be seen.*
NEW YORK ZOOLOGICAL SOCIETY

A *recently hatched* Octopus briareus *is smaller than a penny;
below, a young giant Pacific octopus, seen from above.*

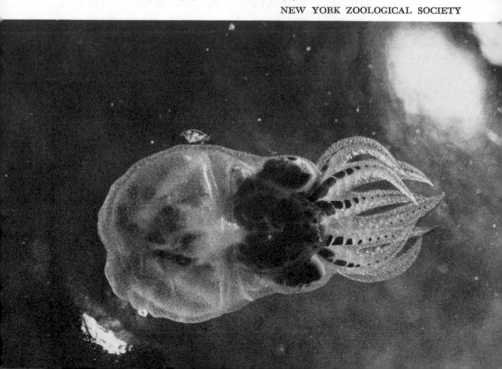

of the females die before the eggs hatch and the rest of them die soon afterward.

One female may lay as many as 50 clusters of eggs. There are about 4000 small octopuses in each cluster. At the moment of birth, the young tear through the tissue that surrounds them and enter the water. They are able to produce squirts of ink immediately. Not all of the eggs hatch at one time, as they are laid over a period of seven or eight days.

The young octopuses face many dangers as they leave their first home. As they come out of the cave, the fish gather around and feast on them. Very few of the thousands of young survive; perhaps two or three live to become adults. The others will become an important part of the food web of the sea.

The young are carried here and there by the ocean currents for about a month. Then, ready to begin adult life, they settle to the bottom.

*Three*

# The Squids, Rockets of the Sea

Squids have the eight arms of the octopus and in addition, two long tentacles, usually ending in broad tips. These tentacles can be drawn back and extended. At the ends of them are suckers with sharp claws on them. Countless whales caught at sea have circular scars left by these destructive suckers.

The body of a squid is a soft tube-shape, with a horizontal fin at the rear and usually side fins; the exact form of these two kinds of fins varies according to the species. The flat rear fin serves as a rudder when the squid wants to jet backward, or to turn and jet forward. The side fins are used for hovering or for slow motion.

Under the mantle is a horny shell which is shaped like a broad blade or a feather pen. It is called a pen and may be 13 millimeters (half an inch) long in the smallest squid and up to 1.3 meters (about four feet) long in the giant squid.

The squid can squirt water either forward or backward through a funnel much like that of the octopus. This makes it possible to dart forward to seize its prey or shoot backward to escape from danger. The shape of a squid's body is ideal for racing through water at high speed. When danger threatens, it can dart off with one squirt in five hundredths of a second. When trying to escape from an enemy, it may squirt an inky fluid into the water, again like the octopus. This hides its movements and confuses the enemy.

When it wants to move fast, a squid moves by jet propulsion from its funnel. The strength of that propulsion astonished the explorer Thor Heyerdahl, who experimen-

*Squids are highly streamlined. This is the common American squid,* Loligo pealeii.

MARINELAND OF FLORIDA

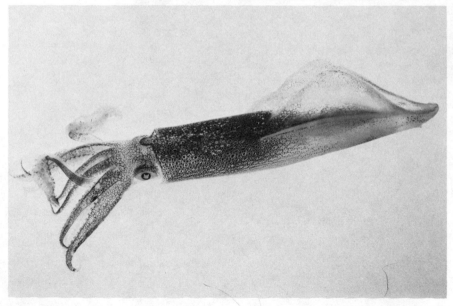

tally crossed the Pacific Ocean on a raft, the *Kon-Tiki*. From his craft he observed certain species of squids taking to the air. He watched close-packed groups jet themselves out of the water and sail through the air like flying fish for at least 45 meters (some 50 yards). They often leaped so high that they landed on the decks of ships. This has been observed now and then by a number of seafarers, as far back as 1880.

Squids live in all the seas of the world. Some are found in the surface waters and others live at depths down to 1.6 kilometers (a mile) or more. They vary in size from giant ones to a midget smaller than a dime. The larger of the more ordinary species roam the open sea, going down to great depths during the day and rising to the surface at night.

### Giants in the Dark

There are truly giant specimens living in the depths of the ocean from 600 to 900 meters (about 2000 to 3000

*It has long been known that squids can squirt an inky fluid into the water when they are threatened by danger, and can also dart off at high speed. What appears to be another kind of reaction has come to light recently in the Atlantic oval squid, shown here. Though in daytime the appearance of a diver near it causes this squid to flee, at night the dark diver's suit conceals the man's size and the squid extends its arms suddenly, which makes it look larger. The "look bigger" defense is used by various water and land animals.* JOHN LIDINGTON

feet) down, where it is cold and dark. They seldom come close to the surface; when they do, the sighting is a rare event. Whalers have reported occasionally seeing a giant squid they judged to be about 18 meters, or some 60 feet, long, including the tentacles, in fierce combat with a sperm whale. These huge squids are a favorite food of this kind of whale. In the struggle the whale usually wins and swallows the squid, though it thereafter carries many imprints of the suckers on its skin. The indigestible horny beaks of the squids lodge in the sperm whales' intestines; there they become coated with a waxy secretion called ambergris, a valuable material used in making perfumes. Masses of ambergris are washed ashore in certain parts of the world.

Scientists have not yet been able to capture one of the giant squids, so to a large extent they remain a secret of the sea.

Some squids are quite small, and we will look at one of them, Spirula, later in a separate chapter. In Japan there is a small four-inch firefly squid. It lives deep down in the sea until mating time, when it comes to the surface. It is covered with color spots and flashes on and off like the firefly after which it is named. It shines so brilliantly that its color changes look like a bursting display of fireworks. There are a number of species of squids that have such luminous color spots, or photophores, as well as various fish, marine worms, and crustaceans. Those photophores that are well developed usually have a lens in front of the source of light and a reflector behind it. The light is pro-

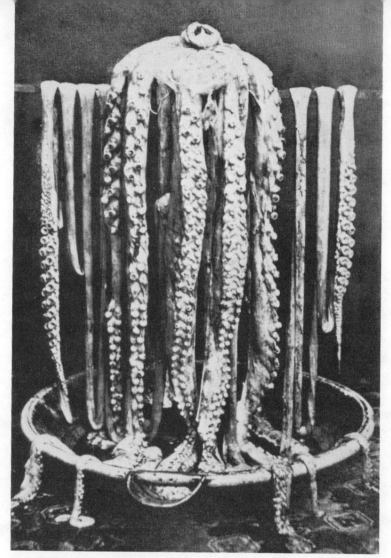

In 1873 the Rev. Moses Harvey of Newfoundland, a naturalist who was interested in "sea monsters," obtained this giant squid from four fishermen and had it photographed, draped over his sponge bath. Until that time many people laughed at the idea that a squid could be so big.

duced by the combination of oxygen with one of two chemicals that come from glands in the animals.

### Color Change and Frenzy

The male squid has a sex arm similar to that of the octopus. On the squid it is the fourth arm on the left. At mating time, the male swims by the side of the female, stroking her with his many arms. As he does this he changes his color repeatedly. The normal color of the squid is a variety of soft rainbow shades. In the excitement of mating, the males become a strong purple. From time to time waves of red and brown appear on their heads and arms.

At mating time, millions of squids gather in one area. Their excited thrashing about at the surface makes the sea appear to be boiling. On the edges of this teeming mob, sharks gather for a feast. They dash in with their jaws wide open and gulp down squids as fast as they can swallow them. Feasting with them are pilot whales, porpoises, and sperm whales.

When a male squid finds a female and embraces her, he quickly slides his sex arm under her mantle to the egg tube. He deposits a packet of sperms and repeats the act several times. In about ten seconds the two separate.

As the excitement dies down both male and female squids are exhausted and sink toward the dark floor of the ocean. The males die soon after hitting the bottom. For three days the females are busy laying very small eggs. They are released in capsules of jelly about a meter

*Female squids lay eggs in capsules, many of which are seen here beneath the animals.*

(some three feet) long. Each capsule contains at least a hundred eggs. The female holds a string of eggs in her arms and goes down to the bottom. She carefully attaches the eggs to a rock or a shell.

When she is finished, she dies. The ocean floor becomes covered with the dead bodies of millions of squids of both sexes. Spawning is the end of life for the smaller species of squid.

In the meantime, the egg capsules become so hard that few predators are interested in them. Only the sea star (sometimes called starfish), which seems to have a very strong constitution, will eat squid embryos, and then only when it can find nothing else to eat.

### The Infant Squid

In about 30 days the embryo is ready to leave the egg and uses jet propulsion to make its exit. Its next act is to shoot out a jet of ink. It almost seems as though it were trying out its accomplishments to see if everything is working properly.

The infant squids look like soft lumps of clear jelly with large eyes. They are born with two tentacles; the eight arms will develop later. Their soft, clear bodies are covered with tiny patches of color—red, yellow, green, black. They look like living jewels as they dart around hunting for food. As they hunt, they are also being hunted. During the first week of their lives, about half of them will be food for other sea creatures. Very few will live to become adults.

The egg case of the female squid is called a mop, because it is made of long, narrow sheaths, each filled with eggs. Each mop contains about 40,000 eggs. When it is crushed it makes a substance that acts like soap, and some people use it for that purpose.

Sometimes a scientist or an amateur naturalist tries to keep captured squids in a tank of sea water, but the animals don't survive long. They are very active creatures and need large areas of water to swim around in. They usually live only a few days in captivity and seem to die of shock—a general drop in the activity of all their body systems. However, one science magazine (see Suggested Reading) presents what may be successful methods of raising them.

*Four*

# Sepia, the Handsome Cuttlefish

The cuttlefish as an animal isn't widely known but its internal shell, called a cuttlebone, is familiar to anyone who has kept a canary. The cuttlebone is a source of salts and lime for caged birds.

Special glands in the mantle contain a liquid that hardens into the cuttlebone, which runs the length of the mantle and strengthens the body of the cuttlefish. Cuttlebones wash up on shore in millions every year.

Like the squid, the cuttlefish has eight short arms and two long tentacles covered with two rows of suckers. The tentacles are broad and flat on the tips. They are used to capture the shrimps and crabs that are their favorite food. When the tentacles are not being used, they are withdrawn into cavities under the eyes.

Like other cephalopods, the cuttlefish—known to scientists as *Sepia officinalis*—has a small black ink sac. This is its main protective device when it is being chased by a whale. An unexpected squirt of ink clouds the water and confuses the whale. Behind this cloud the cuttlefish changes color and quickly escapes by going off in a different direction. Not all cuttlefish, however, are able to escape. One whale that was dissected was found to contain 260 freshly eaten cuttlefish in its stomach and also many beaks from cuttlefish that had already been digested.

## A Flattened Cephalopod

The body of this cephalopod is a departure from that of an octopus or a squid; it is oval-shaped and rather flat. It averages about 15 to 28 centimeters (some six to 11 inches) in length. It rarely grows longer than half a meter (about 20 inches), with the tentacles adding a meter (about 40 inches). One species, however, is only about 75 millimeters (about three inches) long, including the tentacles. The broad upper part of the body is made up of the cuttlebone and is edged with flat, narrow fins on each side. These are used when the cuttlefish is hunting for shrimps and wants to swim slowly.

The cuttlefish has strong jaws shaped like a parrot's beak. It has excellent eyes and probably a wider field of clear vision than we have. It also has a brain that enables it to learn from experience.

The cuttlefish has no home or hole to return to as the octopus does. It hides in the seaweed, but its favorite place is a sandy bottom. This is a good place to hide when it settles down to rest; also, this is where the shrimps hide, half buried in the sand.

Using its fins, the cuttlefish swims slowly just above the sand and shoots out jets of water that uncover a shrimp. The prey may not be noticed at once, but as soon as the shrimp throws more sand over itself it is seized. Small crabs are caught in the same way.

As the cuttlefish draws near its prey, changing colors shimmer across its arms and back. The eight arms stretch out toward the shrimp or crab with color changes flickering over them, but it is the tentacles that shoot out and seize the food. Then it is carried back to the mouth and the beak bites into the flesh. A poisonous salivary fluid quickly kills the prey and the cuttlefish settles down to a meal. Even crab shells are eaten.

## A Quick-Change Artist

The skin of a cuttlefish is usually spotted with white, green, and brown, which makes it almost invisible among the seaweeds. It is the most remarkable of all the cephalopods in its ability to change pattern and color. It does this for two reasons: as a reaction to emotion and to disguise itself against its background of the moment. It is able to produce a great variety of marks, such as black and brown stripes speckled with gold or wavy zigzag lines spreading over its body.

When it is attacked it is likely to turn pale, with just two rounded dark spots on its broad back, like large eyes. This is an effect that probably frightens off some predators. And such is its ability to imitate background that in an experiment it even produced a white rectangle against its darkened back when a rectangular piece of white porcelain was placed near it. When it swims over varying types

*The cuttlefish is rather flat but its streamlined oval form allows a quick getaway from danger, especially when the arms and tentacles are held together in a mass.*

of ocean plants and other objects in shallow water, it reproduces perfectly the color pattern of the sand, rocks, and weeds below it. The change is made almost instantly, taking less than a second.

These beautiful animals are seldom seen. They don't live near the American coasts but are found in the warm coastal waters of the western Pacific, the Mediterranean, and the Indian Ocean. They can be found as far north as England and Scotland, but in these regions they sometimes die in great numbers from a spell of cold weather and their bodies are then found washed up on the beaches.

## Warm-Weather Courtship

The common cuttlefish gather in shallow water to mate during spring and summer. At this time the females are glowing brightly in the darkness as they come to the surface at night. When a female accepts a male, they swim close together, with the male following. In mating, they intertwine their arms and remain in a close embrace for two to five minutes. The male's specialized sex arm places the sperm packet on the sperm receptacle of the female. This is on a groove near her mouth.

The quarter-inch-long eggs are laid one at a time and pass through the sperm receptacle of the female. The eggs are fertilized and covered with a secretion that forms a tough capsule which is darkened by ink from the ink sac. The female may lay from 250 to 300 eggs and fastens each one to a bit of seaweed or some other support.

A young cuttlefish is about 1.5 millimeters (approximately a half inch) long when it is born, and may live four or five years, though its life span is uncertain. It has an ink sac and will use it within the first minute of life if it is disturbed. The young dart around hunting for food almost immediately. Their food is newborn prawns and other shrimps, crabs, and fish.

*Five*

# The Pearly Nautilus

The ancient nautiloids had coiled shells with chambers. They have nearly all disappeared except for one fairly common type, the pearly nautilus. This animal swims in our oceans as a "living fossil." It is a deep-sea cephalopod and has been caught as far down as 660 meters (about 2000 feet). It is one of the oldest kinds of animal living on earth.

There are six species of the pearly nautilus living today. These are all that remain of the 3000 or so species of the nautiloids which left their fossil records in rock millions of years ago.

In ages past, uncounted nautiloids filled the seas of the world. Today the pearly nautiluses are found in most abundance in the warm waters between Australia and the Philippines. They have earned the name of living fossils because their shells appear to be a perfect copy of the ancient fossils. But they are miniatures, for some of those fossil shells measure five meters (about 16 feet) across, while the modern nautilus shell is no wider than 10 inches. The nautilus has been a mystery since it was first discovered. Scientists know very little about its living habits or its life cycle.

## Pearly Shell and Swaying Arms

How does a nautilus look as it goes about its underwater life? The creamy white shell, streaked with rich reddish-brown bands, rides gently just above the muddy bottom of the ocean. From the large opening at the front of the shell the face protrudes, and a thick cluster of 50 to 90 arms moves slowly about.

The swaying arms sniff for the odor of food. If it finds nothing, the animal may expel a jet of water that carries it rapidly backward. When it reaches an area where clumps of greenish seaweed cover the floor, it may slow down, since this is a good place for finding food.

As the nautilus moves along slowly, the stretched-out arms may touch something, and two of them quickly twine around a crab, lobster, or fish. The prey is brought to its mouth and torn apart by its horny beak. The nautilus quickly eats its meal and then floats away on another hunt.

The nautilus has two large eyes on short stalks. In the hunt for food it is the arms that carry organs for smelling out the prey. These arms don't have suckers like those of other cephalopods; instead the tips are covered with a sticky substance.

Jacques Cousteau, a noted authority on ocean life, has brought us many stimulating films about sea animals, and one shows the nautilus swimming free in the ocean. It is a graceful animal in an elegant and beautiful shell. Efforts have been made to raise these creatures in public aquariums but in most cases they die in a few days.

The eggs of the nautilus are laid one at a time and are attached to rocks or seaweed. When it is first hatched, the female has a very small shell; males never have shells. When the body and the shell both grow a size larger, the nautilus seals off the small, empty chamber with a delicate pearly partition and moves forward, like its nautiloid ancestors.

The animal connects the empty chamber with the new chamber by a small tube that comes through the partition. This tube is a part of its body. As the young nautilus continues to grow, it continues to move another space forward and seal off another empty chamber, each time extending the connecting tube.

There may be 25 or 30 sealed-off chambers before the growing is complete; thus this cephalopod is sometimes called the chambered nautilus. The animal secretes a gas which passes into the empty chambers through the tube. The gas helps to keep the shell afloat. By making more gas or letting some out, it can regulate the buoyancy of the shell, and so rise toward the surface or sink to the bottom at will. It also moves horizontally by rapid jet propulsion.

### A Shell Home

The shell with its curved partitions is a superb piece of natural art. When it is cut in half, the chambers are revealed. The animal lives at the mouth of the last chamber

and the shell is her permanent home. She can swim out-
side of the shell but can't leave it because her body is a
part of it. The inside of her home is lined with glistening
mother-of-pearl. The shell is very thin and is a favorite
material of craftsmen.

When it wants to, the female nautilus can withdraw

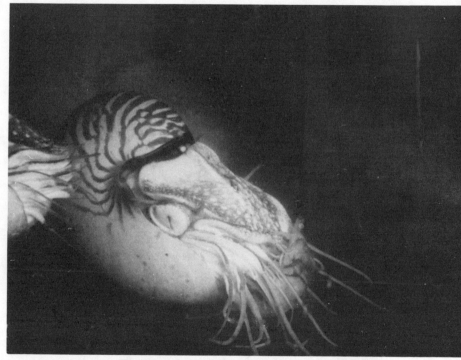

DR. NORINE HAVEN, HOPKINS MARINE STATION

*An adult pearly nautilus,* Nautilus pompilius, *feeding in an
aquarium. It grasps the food, a piece of fish seen just below
its hood, in its tentacles and bites off pieces with its beak.*

completely into this shell. A brown leathery hood comes forward and closes the opening, offering a certain amount of protection. However, the nautilus often becomes food for large sea turtles. Unlike other cephalopods, it has no ink sac to create a black cloud. Nor is it able to struggle against the wave forces of the sea itself. If the animal comes too near the surface, high waves may throw it against the corals or wash it up on the beach. The shell breaks easily.

The large number of arms can be something of a problem. If the nautilus is disturbed, or senses danger, she first withdraws some of the way into the shell, doing this by bringing the arms partially in and arranging them together in a close fit. Then if it becomes necessary, she can retract them quickly and completely and finish by closing the opening with the hood.

### Moving by Jets

The body of the nautilus is covered by a strong mantle. When the muscles force the open mantle tightly against the head, it can expel water through the funnel, producing jet propulsion. At one time it was thought that this cephalopod used its arms for crawling about on the bottom. Some of the older books show drawings of it creeping on its arms, but this has been definitely disproved. The jet propulsion is its only means of moving.

During the day a nautilus remains deep in the water from about 150 to 300 meters (approximately 500 to 1000 feet) below the surface. Its shell touches or almost touches

DR. NORINE HAVEN, HOPKINS MARINE STATION

*A* juvenile *Nautilus* pompilius. *The last chamber area of the adult's shell is white, but young nautiluses have stripes in that portion too. A small part of the funnel, or siphon, protrudes at the front of the shell, beneath the tentacles.*

the sea bottom, and its hood is nearly closed. About half an hour before sunset it becomes active and rises to approximately 65 meters (about 200 feet) from the surface to feed. In moving about after food, it raises the hood above the shell enough to expose its eyes and arms.

In early summer, fishermen drop nets or wicker baskets

to capture these animals. The meat is sold in the market places as food and the shells are bought by craftsmen. Jewelry, spoons, buttons, and many other ornaments are made from them and sold in curio shops. Thousands of shells are cleaned and sent to clearing centers in the cities of Zamboanga and Manila, in the Philippines. Commercial greed seems to be the biggest threat to the nautilus and its continued existence.

The nautilus lives about eight to 12 years. When it dies, the empty shell often comes to the surface and floats about until waves wash it up on the shore. Meanwhile thousands of young are hatching in the sea and growing toward adulthood.

*Six*

# The Argonaut,
# an Octopus with a Shell

The paper nautilus, or argonaut, is actually a free-swimming octopus. It was misnamed a nautilus many years ago and the name clung to it.

The argonaut animal looks much like other octopuses but it isn't like them in its way of life. It has eight arms and a pair of eyes somewhat resembling those of vertebrates. The eyes seem very expressive as they look out from between the protecting arms; it is easy to imagine they suggest shyness.

The female makes a lovely shell but it doesn't have chambers in it as the nautilus shell does. Neither is the argonaut attached bodily to her shell. The male does not make any shell.

The female has a pair of very specialized arms that are shaped like paddles. These arms give off a limy substance that develops into a thin, delicately scalloped shell. The arms clasp the two sides of the shell while depositing more of the limy material, increasing the shell's size.

There is no connection at all between the shell and the animal. The arms simply hold this casing in place. The shell is thin as tissue paper; the color is a silvery white with a bit of brown at the coiled end. It is about 10 to 15 centimeters (about four to six inches) wide, and is both a home and an egg case. The female lays her eggs in the back coil of the shell.

## A Special Tentacle

The male, seldom more than half an inch long, has a specialized tentacle that is used in reproduction. A slender threadlike growth appears at the tip of this tentacle; it contains the sperms. At mating time the end of it is inserted in the female's mantle cavity and breaks off. The sperms are released and will fertilize the eggs as they are being laid. When all the sperm cells have been used, the tentacle is discarded.

In some cases the tentacle breaks off from the male before a female is available and it then swims about vigorously as if it were a whole animal itself until a female is reached.

The argonaut lays several thousand eggs in the shell egg case and remains there brooding and protecting them. Sometimes the male occupies the shell with the female and her eggs.

If the female leaves the egg case at any time, she carries it with her in her two front arms. She retires into it when she is disturbed and lives with it until she dies. This is

*A female argonaut out of its shell, at left. The two broad arms produce a substance that develops into this covering. Because the shell is so thin and fragile, the argonaut is sometimes miscalled a "paper nautilus."*

shortly after the eggs hatch. If the shell is lost, she apparently can't make a new one, but she can mend holes in it.

### The Fragile Shell

The shells are so fragile that it is rare to find a perfect specimen on the beach. When they are washed ashore by heavy waves, they are usually broken by the waves that

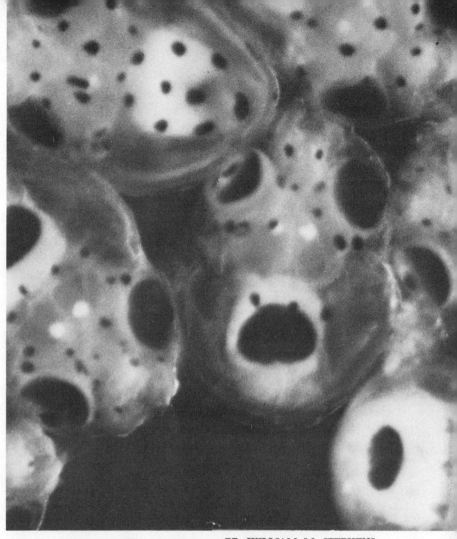

DR. WILLIAM M. STEPHENS

*Infant argonauts, each about one millimeter long. The paired dark circular spots on each are the developing eyes.*

*Left: The argonaut's shell is also an egg case. Fingertips give a clear idea of the animal's size, though some shells are bigger than this one.* DR. WILLIAM M. STEPHENS

follow. They are completely different from the more familiar mollusk shells, such as those of oysters or clams, being so fragile, and quite unattached to the animal. An oyster or clam will die if it is separated from its shell.

The argonaut is seldom seen alive. It is totally pelagic —that is, lives in the open sea away from the shore—and usually drifts in the water rather than swims. Normally it lives its entire life without contact with land or the sea floor. As it drifts along, it feeds on plankton and other minute animals and plants of the sea.

The argonaut is a beautiful little creature. It glows constantly in a rainbow of colors from yellow-orange to blue-green and violet, with shades of brown. It is a rare treat to see the living animal swimming in a blue-green sea.

*Seven*

# Little Spirula

Spirula is a primitive deep-sea squid that is still living today and is closely related to the cuttlefish. Inside its body is a small coiled shell that sticks out of the body a little on opposite sides at the rear end. The shell is a pearly tube about 25 millimeters (an inch) across. It has many chambers, 25 to 37, each with a glistening mother-of-pearl partition.

For centuries these shells, sometimes called ram's-horn shells, were found on beaches in great numbers without giving any idea of what the animal itself is like. Even as recently as 1921, only about 12 specimens of the little squid itself had been collected from all over the world, and these were damaged by the action of waves or by decay. Finally a Danish biologist who was tracking down something else—eels—brought up many living spirulas in his nets, and they began to be better understood.

The spirula is one of the smallest cephalopods, seldom more than 3.5 centimeters (about one and a half inches) long, including the arms. Although it is so very small, it has a beak that can deliver a powerful bite.

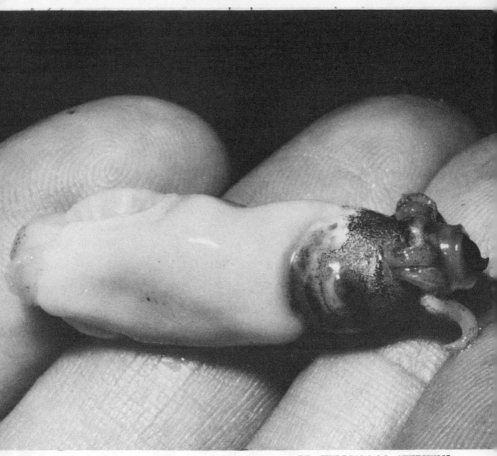

DR. WILLIAM M. STEPHENS

*A spirula is one of the smallest squids, and is seldom seen, though its shell can sometimes be found by the thousands on beaches. The shell, which is inside the live animal, protrudes a bit on two sides, as can be seen near its rear end.*

## A Strange Position

Its soft body has the eight arms and the two tentacles of the squid and the cuttlefish. But unlike the others, a spirula spends its entire life hanging head down in the water. Because of its position, it travels up and down through about 180 to 2000 meters (about 600 to 6500 feet) of sea water. It has been found at depths of about five and a half kilometers, or three and a half miles. Though it is a deep-sea animal, it can stand the release of the terrible deep-water pressure when it is brought up to the surface.

Spirula has two small end-fins that aid in its swimming. Between the fins is a light organ that glows continuously with a yellowish-green light, which perhaps helps to keep a group together.

Spirula lives in the open ocean throughout tropical and subtropical seas. When it is caught in a trap or brought up in a net, it usually appears to be dead. But it is ordinarily only "pretending"; if it is left alone it generally comes to life. When it is disturbed, it can withdraw its head, arms, and tentacles into the mantle cavity and close the opening. The tough and slippery mantle offers good protection.

When the animal dies, the shell floats to the surface. Sometimes the beaches are covered with thousands of these little shells. They are buffeted by the winds and carried by the ocean currents until they are washed up on shores hundreds or even thousands of miles from their home areas. They have been found on the beaches of all five continents. By holding a shell to the light, one can see the many chambers—a reminder that its ancestor was an ammonoid.

# Eight
# The Ancient Ammonoids

Far back in the past, a period for which our only information comes from fossils in the rocks, there was another group of cephalopods called ammonoids (or sometimes ammonites). They too, like the nautiloids, kept sealing off their former living space in their external shell until finally there were many small "rooms" behind them. Their name came from the ancient Egyptian sun god Ammon, which had a ram's head with curled horns.

Ammonoids varied in size from 13 millimeters (half an inch) in diameter to huge shells that sometimes measured almost three meters (about 10 feet) across. They reached the peak of their development some two hundred million years ago.

These magnificent animals became extinct about 80 million years ago. Although there were about 5000 species of them, none survived. The fossils of the ammonoids are very common and easily found. Collectors have called them "serpent stones" because they resemble the petrified remains of coiled snakes.

We can be very glad that all the cephalopods haven't

*A fossil ammonoid, a cephalopod that became extinct about 80 million years ago. The lines suggesting frilly leaves are suture lines, where the walls of new chambers were joined to the shell.*

become extinct, like the ammonoids and most of the nautiloids. Certainly the oceans would be less interesting if these strange and often beautiful creatures were not among their inhabitants.

# Suggested Reading

## Books

Joseph Cook and William L. Wisner, *The Phantom World of the Octopus and Squid* (Dodd, Mead, 1965)

Jacques-Yves Cousteau and Philippe Diolé, *Octopus and Squid: The Soft Intelligence* (Doubleday, 1973)

Olive Earle, *Octopus* (Morrow, 1955)

Alister Hardy, *The Open Sea: The World of Plankton* (Houghton Mifflin, 1956; contains information on octopuses, squids, cuttlefishes, spirulas, nautiluses)

Alice L. Hopf, *Biography of an Octopus* (Putnam, 1971)

C. P. Idyll, *Abyss* (Crowell, 1964; contains a chapter on octopuses and squids)

Marie M. Jenkins, *The Curious Mollusks* (Holiday House, 1972)

William Stephens, *Southern Seashores* (Holiday House, 1968; contains information on argonauts and spirulas)

## Magazine Articles

B. B. Boycott, "Learning in the Octopus," *Scientific American*, March 1965

G. W. Compton, "Argonaut Octopus: Rare Find from the Sea," *Science Digest*, July 1970

J. Coulon, "Hunting Demons from Hell: Giant Squids in Newfoundland Waters," *Science News*, July 12, 1969

Jacques-Yves Cousteau and Philippe Diolé, "Last Dance on the Mating Ground" (octopuses and squids), *Natural History*, April 1973

"Deadly Octopus Plague," *Science News*, July 12, 1969

Walter Deas, "Venomous Octopus," *Sea Frontiers*, Nov.–Dec. 1970

"How To Raise a Squid," *Science Digest*, April 1970

"Mating Games Octopi Play," *Life*, Nov. 6, 1970

"One Octopus Brain Has Two Memory Stores," *Science News Letter*, March 27, 1965

S. Schlee, "Prince Albert's Way of Catching a Squid," *Natural History*, Feb. 1970

Ken N. Sokolski, with notes by Jerome Lettvin, "The Annotated Octopus," *Natural History*, Nov. 1969

G. L. Voss and R. F. Sisson, "Squids: Jet-Powered Torpedoes of the Deep," *National Geographic*, March 1967

———, "Shy Monster, the Octopus," *National Geographic*, Dec. 1971

Martin J. Wells, "Invertebrate Learning," *Natural History*, Feb. 1966

———, "Memory Traces in the Octopus," *Sea Frontiers*, Sept. 1969

F. G. Wood and J. F. Gennaro, "Octopus Trilogy," *Natural History*, March 1971

W. Zeiller and G. Compton, "Rare Gift from the Sea" (argonaut), *Sea Frontiers*, Nov. 1970

# Index